Yellow

Julie Brown

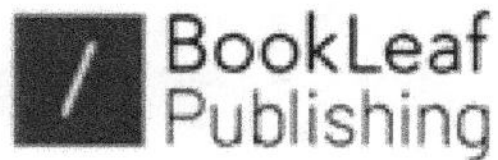

Presentation by *BookLeaf Publishing*

Web: www.bookleafpub.com

E-mail: info@bookleafpub.com

ISBN: 9789357210874

First edition 2022

DEDICATION

For my lovely daughter x

ACKNOWLEDGEMENT

Thanks to Lydia for this amazing gift!

PREFACE

My thoughts in poems

Cookie

Don't stop let it out
I don't want to sing or shout
Don't fit, mustn't fit
I'm never far out of it
Wind up, pull it through
Omg isn't that cool
Let's start, never stop
I'm going to hit that
Man I want a cookie
Man I want a cookie

Stepladder

It was put out to protect, to alert and keep safe.
Guarding a cracked manhole cover was it's job.
However it was stolen and, taken in the night.
Maybe Liam Neeson can help return our
stepladder and avoid a fight?

JOMD

The job of my dreams is coming soon, I've got it and can't wait to start. I love what I do and want to be the boss to ensure successful market access. It is sometimes hard to explain what I do but without it our products may never get to you...

On the top

There is a long way down
But I not frown
I reach higher and try to find
The extra we look for to grow

School

I look out the window and fall asleep
Then some creep shouts 'miss she has fallen
asleep
I wake up find the class is screaming behind
Every day is the same the class is unruly and the
teacher does complain...

My future

My future, my hope
My love, my scope
My possibilities, my world
My beauty, my life

Lyd

Smart, beautiful, funny and caring
Always thinking, always so capable
Wonderful, imaginative, responsible and fun
The best, kindest, my lovely one x

Small Cat

Waiting at the door, where is my food
Come on people, I'm not being rude
I know you can see me, you are going to let me
in. Come on I'm hungry, I'm getting thin!

Watch

Full of tech, with so many options
Not just the time but also a vast expanse
You forget to wear me and you lose my skills
I support your life and give you thrills.

Car

I'm waiting, it has been ordered
But alas a delay, it will be delivered
But not today.

Mirror

I love looking at myself
What I'm wearing, how I'm staring
Just me and no one else.

Room

Boxes, things, too many to count
In my head I organise, I find a way out.

Daily Intake

Each day I must take my A-Z,
I believed my body needs it
But it is just expensive pee.

Beauty

I invest to find it
I buy, I invest
I chase it daily and I never rest

Foxy

I hear them at night
Strange noises and maybe a fight
I have seen a few
These smart, beautiful creatures who are always
on cue.

Thank you...

I say thank you whenever I'm complemented
I am grateful and was taught to express it
My thanks are sincere and I often will say thank
you, as I hear well done anyway.

Weight

I'm overweight and maybe obese
It is hard not to think of food and diets bring
little relief. Sticking at it is the hardest trial
because I have cakes in the freezer it is like I'm
set up to fail

Yellow

It is the best colour
So bright, so energetic
I want a yellow Porsche
But I'm yet to get it

www.ingramcontent.com/pod-product-compliance
Lightning Source LLC
LaVergne TN
LVHW021355200726
843509LV00014B/2864